D1482679

The Soul Discovery
COLORING BOOK

Noodle, Doodle, and Scribble Your Way
to an Extraordinary Life

JANET CONNER

ILLUSTRATED BY CHRISTINE PENSA AND YOU!

Conari Press

This edition first published in 2016 by Conari Press, an imprint of
Red Wheel/Weiser, LLC
With offices at:
65 Parker Street, Suite 7
Newburyport, MA 01950
www.redwheelweiser.com

Copyright © 2016 by Janet Conner and Christine Pensa
All rights reserved. No part of this publication may be reproduced or transmitted
in any form or by any means, electronic or mechanical, including photocopying,
recording, or by any information storage and retrieval system, without permission
in writing from Red Wheel/Weiser, LLC. Reviewers may quote brief passages.

ISBN: 978-1-57324-685-9

Library of Congress Control Number: 2016930245

Cover design by Jim Warner
Cover art © Christine Pensa
Interior by Christine Pensa
Typeset in Nueva and Cantoria

Printed in the United States of America
M&G

10 9   8 7 6 5 4 3 2 1

BEFORE

Before you contemplate the first question . . .
Before you pick up your favorite pen and start soul writing . . .
Before you grab that cobalt blue pencil jumping up and down in the box . . .

Before you do anything with this delight-filled coloring book, let's talk for a moment about the sacred intention of this book.

The subtitle holds a clue: *Noodle, Doodle, and Scribble Your Way to an Extraordinary Life.* We'll get to the noodling, doodling, and scribbling bits, and coloring and soul writing, too. But first, look at where this adventure is headed: an extraordinary life.

What is that? What is an *extraordinary* life?

The first thought that comes to mind for most of us is a life filled with all the things we label success: career, recognition, house, relationship, income.

But your extraordinary life isn't something *out there*. It isn't something to search for, or try to build, or set out to achieve. It isn't even something you create—not from your logical conscious mind, anyway.

Does that mean your extraordinary life isn't real? Heavens, no! Your extraordinary life is more real than all those definitions of success you've been given. But, here's your first *Aha!*—and it's a big one: You can't find your extraordinary life out there because your extraordinary life is in here.

It's not something you search for; it's something you *listen* for.
It's not something you seek; it's something you *see*.
It's not something you build; it's something you *nurture*.
It's not something you achieve; it's something you *discover.*

And when you do, you will fall madly in love with the life your heart has been longing for—the extraordinary life waiting within. Waiting to be seen, nurtured, and loved.

How are you going to discover it? That's where all the fun comes in.

Christine Pensa

your Discovery team

This collaborative book is an invitation to make *heart art*. An invitation to deepen your connection with your child's view of creativity and let go of your adult judgement of what art should be. This kind of creating is not about making something the *right way*. This is a creative exploration where you allow your he*ART* to take the lead.

As a child, I created freely. I found comfort and peace drawing and creating in my little bubble of light. Then I came up against judgement, my own and others', and I walked away for twenty years. My journey back to my original freedom of expression has been one of the great delights of my life. That's why being part of this very special book of discovery with Janet is so exciting for me. I want to invite you to begin (or deepen) the journey to your creative he*ART*. As Toltec wisdom teaches, each person's life is art, and you create each day upon your canvas, choosing to live colourfully and vibrantly with an unlimited palette—or not. I believe making art is a *portal to understanding your own power to create and change your life*.

I *know* exploring your world and your creative soul should be a *joy*—full of laughter and fun. Essential to the creative explorer is a sense of humour. I learned that one from experience. You too can join Janet and me to become a creative explorer journeying to parts of your own expression you haven't visited in some time—or ever!

This book is an invitation to deepen your experience of making art through play. Our intention for this book is to help you begin to access the art-making language of your soul, allowing you to express the promptings of *your colour-filled heart*.

Part of you longs to be heard with your eyes. Come, play!

What do you mean by . . . scribbling?
To scribble is to let go of making a picture. It's an invitation to feel. What lines do you want to make—soft and flowing, or hard and jagged? Do you want to press down hard on your paper or gently dust the surface?

What do you mean by . . . doodling?
Channel the kid who got in trouble for doodling on textbooks in class. Doodling feels loose and flowing, but you're also trying to find rough images here. Let something emerge.

Colouring pages
These pages are meant as an opportunity to meditate on the questions and inspire *your own* art making. Use the colours and mediums* that delight you, and feel free to add your own images in the blank spaces.
I have created a special web page filled with colouring ideas and videos at www.artthatmoves.ca.

What do you mean by . . . scribble-drawing?
This is an invitation to keep it loose. Let yourself explore judgement-free creating by creating what *your heart* wants to express here.

Some tips . . .
Begin the *Creative Prompts* by placing both feet on the ground and breathing deeply.

Invite yourself to become an observer. Pay attention to the colours you choose and why. ecome an observer of life. Invite colours and images into your life in a new way.

Pay attention to the feel of your crayon, pencil, pen, or marker on your paper. Get to know what *medium** feels good for you in that moment.

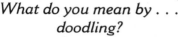

*medium = what artists use to create their art

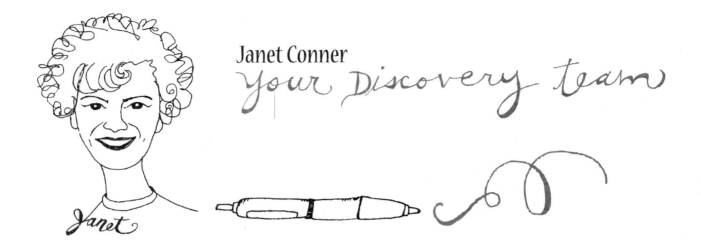

Janet Conner

your Discovery team

Extraordinary life? I didn't have a clue what that was or how to find it. Like so many, I spent my thirties and forties working hard to build the great American success story with an executive title, downtown office, suburban home, and handsome husband. When it all imploded, I found myself sobbing in my living room, scared, broke, and lost.

On a particularly dark day, I had my first taste of just how extraordinary life can be. I needed help and help was on the way. My puppy wrestled a big book off the shelf and dragged it to me. Startled, I sat and began to read. In the first few pages, I read that you can access a source of wisdom through writing. I threw down the book, grabbed a pen, wrote *Dear God*, and began a lifelong conversation with a loving, wise Voice.

Following the wisdom of my Voice, I have discovered a most extraordinary life filled with wonder and joy at every turn. One of my great joys is writing books. My first, *Writing Down Your Soul*, shared deep soul writing with the world. You want an extraordinary *life*? Begin by activating your extraordinary *Voice*!

It's surprisingly easy. Practice the following seven steps and your writing will slip effortlessly out of journaling and into dialogue with a divine presence. In brain science terms, you are moving out of speedy beta brain waves into slow, creative theta waves. In soul terminology, you are exiting the constraints of your logical conscious mind and stepping into the vast realms of the soul.

This is where the magic is. This is where your extraordinary life is. Come, play!

Seven Steps to Soul Writing

ONE

Intention has creative power. **Set your intention** to go deep and connect with the Voice with a thought, movement, or blessing.

TWO

You are speaking to something within you that is greater than you. **Address the Voice** by name. Don't have a name? Try *Dear Friend, Dear Beloved, Dear Voice*…. Your special name will come.

THREE

The computer is wonderful, but to feel the living presence of the Voice *in* your pen and *in* your body, **write by hand.**

FOUR

Activate all 5 senses. Vision and touch are automatic. So is hearing; your brain hears when you write. For smell, light a candle or sniff essential oils. That leaves taste. A Navajo shaman taught me to drink water mindfully at the end of a ceremony to bring the blessings into my whole body. When you finish soul writing, sip a glass of water, drinking in all the wisdom and grace you received.

FIVE

Ask lots of questions. Questions are the magic that activates the Voice. Ask open-ended, big, deep, (even scary) questions!

SIX

Write fast. When you write full speed ahead, you leave your conscious mind sputtering in the distance and the Voice has a chance to break through. Grammar, handwriting, logic…who cares!

SEVEN

Be grateful. When you lift your glass, say thank you. Because you were heard.

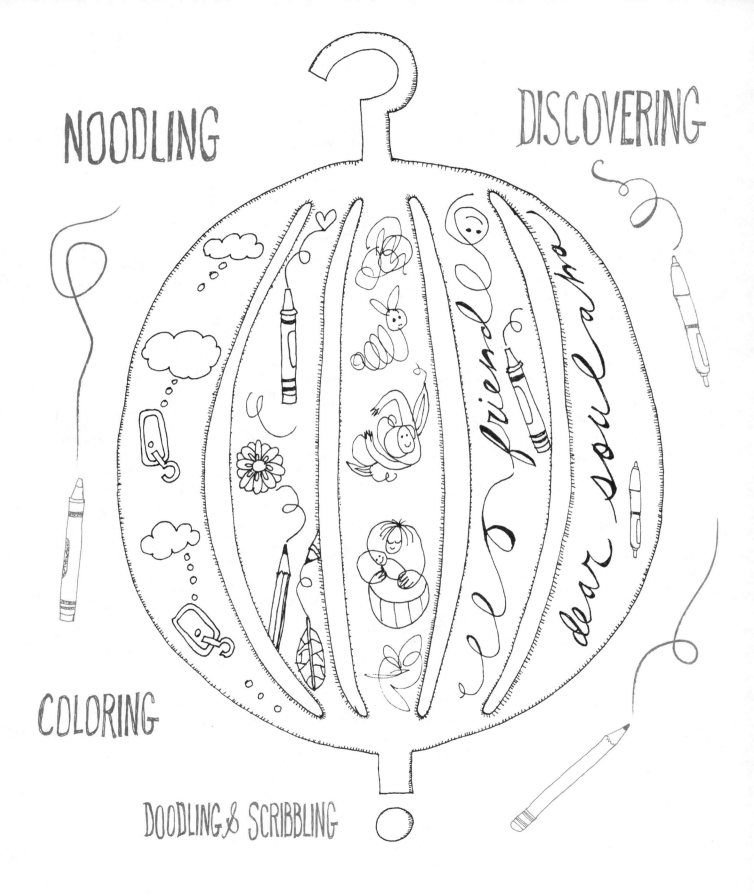

NOODLING

DISCOVERING

COLORING

DOODLING & SCRIBBLING

Your Discovery explorations

The soul doesn't get too excited by facts and logic. She loves stories, symbols, myths, music, color, light, and nature. And she loves questions—the bigger and juicier the better. Questions send your soul flying below the conscious mind and into a treasure trove of creativity, truth, and beauty called the *imaginal realm*. This unusual coloring book is designed to help you and your soul drop out of the conscious mind and into the imaginal realm, where you will discover what is true and beautiful for you. It all takes place in an *imaginal garden*, the perfect place to discover your extraordinary life.

There are 22 adventures with 6 exploration pages for each:

Page 1

Read Janet's **Question** and **Story**. Then, do a little **Noodling** on the chair. Don't try to answer the question, just reflect for a bit; allow whatever wants to surface to surface.

Page 2

Play with the Creative Prompt from Christine on the **Doodling & Scribbling** page. Don't worry about what you're doing or how it looks. Let your soul play!

Page 3

Enjoy Christine's delightful **Coloring** page. Let your soul choose the colors. You may be surprised by what she loves. And please, color outside the lines! And add anything your heart desires.

Page 4

Add **Soul Writing** to your **Doodling & Scribbling**. Janet created a writing suggestion, but don't feel limited by it. Let your soul take the lead.

Page 5

The whole time you've been noodling, doodling, scribbling, and soul writing, your soul has been **Discovering.** Record your **Aha!** and drink it into your whole being.

Page 6

Does your soul want more room? Give her the blank page.

Enough talking, let's play!

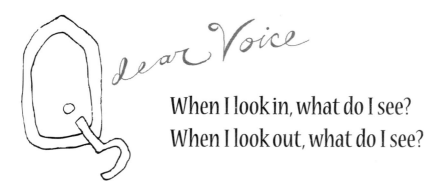

Dear Voice

1

When I look in, what do I see?
When I look out, what do I see?

I taught deep soul writing in Portland, Oregon, the summer of 2011. I stayed with my brother Larry, who has a beautiful spiritual library. Poking through his books, I found two on icons. I was startled to learn that icons are not art; they are instruments of prayer. That's why the eyes don't match. One looks out at you and one gazes inward, drawing you to the divine. I grabbed a pen: *Dear God, I want an icon!* A week later, I got my first peek at the cover for *My Soul Pages*. The owl stared at me. I stared at the owl. The eyes didn't match! No wonder we love soul writing under the wise, loving eyes of the owl; it's an icon. Well, guess what, you are an icon, too. Look in a mirror and see for yourself. So, what do you see when you look out? What do you see when you look in?

NOODLING

DOODLING & SCRIBBLING

CREATIVE *prompt*

Choose one colour for your inner eye
and one for your outer seeing eye.
Holding your crayons, soft pencils, or
markers in both hands, close your eyes
and let yourself scribble-draw for 20 seconds.
Open your eyes and observe what
you have drawn. Doodle, adding any
colours, lines, or words that come.
Just allow.

COLORING

DOODLING & SCRIBBLING
Soul Writing

hmm ...

Look at a situation with your outward eye.

Now, look at it with your inward eye.

Is there a difference?

Dear friend,

Aha!

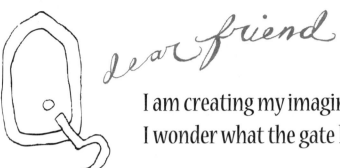

dear friend

2

I am creating my imaginal garden in my heart.
I wonder what the gate looks like ...

A gate is so interesting. With one voice, it says *Keep out*. With the other, it whispers *Come in*. As you walk past, you wonder, *What's behind that gate?* You have gates, too. Some elegant, some warm, some a tad on the scary side. Sometimes you open a gate and let people in. Sometimes people yank and let themselves in! Some gates have been locked so long, you forgot you closed them. Your extraordinary life has a gate, too. And only you can design it. It can be as simple or as elaborate as you like. It can be tall and secretive or short and inviting. It can be wacky and fun. Or it can be so otherworldly, it redefines *gate* altogether. Create a gate that feels like you. Then, the real adventure begins. You have to open it *not knowing what's on the other side*.

NOODLING

DOODLING & SCRIBBLING

CREATIVE prompt

Imaginal gates don't have to look like gates. If you would like to see what your own gate looks like, place your feet on the ground and close your eyes. Breathe deeply and scirbble for 5 seconds. Let go. Open your eyes and allow yourself to play by doodling for 5 minutes. See if your gate emerges.

More: Name your imaginal garden and draw a sign for it.

COLORING

DOODLING & SCRIBBLING
Soul Writing

open sesame

Need some strength to open your gate?
Speak this invocation:
I am here.
I am present.
I am open.
I am ready.

DISCOVERING

dear Voice

When the gate opens, and my heart starts singing, and my imagination flies everywhere it wants to go, what wonders do I see?

When you open the gate into the garden of your Extraordinary Life, what do you see? You can see anything, you know. Because here, anything is possible—and everything is real. You can have magical trees with tree houses, purple ponds with turquoise fish, fountains spewing rosewater, trellises dripping gold. You can have the sun *and* the moon—day and night at once! You can even build a secret shed for writing and painting, dancing and dreaming. In the garden of *my* extraordinary life, Owls blink wisdom, Ospreys drop treasures, Rocks talk, and Books grow on trees! And the angel of beauty reigns over all. Who or what wants to be in *your* garden? What do you see when your heart opens and reveals the extraordinary image of your extraordinary life?

NOODLING

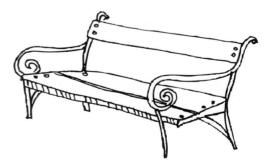

DOODLING & SCRIBBLING

CREATIVE *prompt*

Doodle, sketch, or, if you prefer, cut out images
from a magazine to collage your favourite
corner in your garden. Pay attention to what
colour is most important to nurture yourself
in your imaginal garden. What textures are best
for you here? Where are the places you sit, dance,
meditate, or dream here?
*Hint: Think Dr. Seuss meets the Dalai Lama
meets your soul's desire.*

COLORING

DOODLING & SCRIBBLING
Soul Writing

oh my ...

How does it *feel* to be in your garden?
Everything and everyone in this magical place knows you.
The garden has always known you were coming.
It is now welcoming you home!

DISCOVERING

Dear soul

Aha!

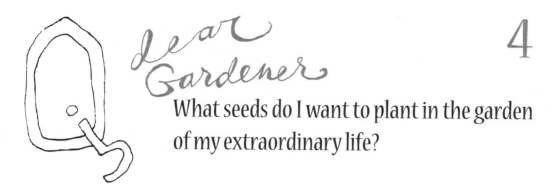

dear Gardener

4

What seeds do I want to plant in the garden of my extraordinary life?

In spring the air is alive with possibility. You can feel it. Why, you can smell it. The heart quickens with desire to begin afresh and you rush outside to plunge your hands in the dirt. In your imaginal garden it's spring, too—time to till your soil and plant your seeds. But which seeds? This is a do-it-yourself life; no landscaper can choose or plan or plant for you. So, off to the Extraordinary Seed Store you go! Take your time considering the possibilities. What do you want to flourish in your life: quiet, simplicity, loving relationships, a peaceful home, clarity of purpose, delightful creativity, joyful work, restful sleep, time to study, time to play, fertile partnerships, spiritual practice, divine connection…? What do you long for? What do you love? What will bring you joy?

NOODLING.

Extraordinary Life Seeds

DOODLING & SCRIBBLING

CREATIVE prompt

Close your eyes and scribble-draw for 5 seconds holding this intention: I clearly see what new growth is inside the perfect seed I will plant for myself today. Open your eyes and continue to doodle what comes to you. Add colour or words to describe your seed.

More: Create a seed packet for your seed. Name it and illustrate the cover of the packet.

COLORING

DOODLING & SCRIBBLING
Soul Writing

my soil

I love my seeds.
Now, how shall I prepare my soul—
oops, I mean soil—
for my beautiful life?

DISCOVERING

Dear friend?

Aha!

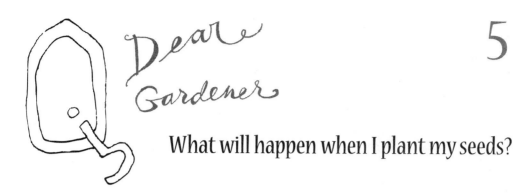

Dear Gardener

5

What will happen when I plant my seeds?

With soil prepped and Extraordinary Seeds in your hands, you are ready to plant your garden. Have you ever considered the miracle that is a seed? How can something so tiny grow into waist-high sunflowers? How does a half-inch acorn become a stately oak tree? For that matter, how does one fertilized egg cell grow into you or me?! The seed knows *what* it is to be and it knows *how* to grow into that. But first, she must wait in the dark. Everything and everyone begins in the dark. When the seed senses the time is ripe, she sends up an etheric leaf, a tiny energetic imprint of her leaf-to-be. The actual green leaf follows, filling in the invisible outline with cellulose and chlorophyll and the pulse of life. What etheric "leaves" are you sending up through the dark?

NOODLING

DOODLING & SCRIBBLING

CREATIVE *prompt*

In the center of your paper draw
your tiny seed. Draw five or more
concentric circles around your seed.
Choose your colours and textures
mindfully. What will best nurture your
seed and the etheric plant it is becoming?
Be gentle with your movements.
More: Draw the etheric plant that will
spring from your seed. Give it a name.

COLORING

DOODLING & SCRIBBLING
Soul Writing

could be ...

If these are *extraordinary* seeds
that send up *extraordinary* images
of what could be…
then, what could be?

DISCOVERING

Dear? Beloved

Aha!

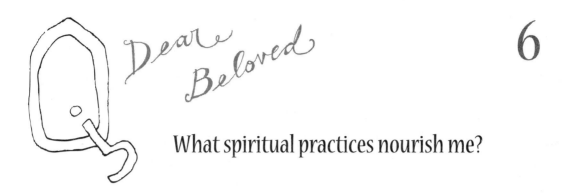

Dear Beloved

What spiritual practices nourish me?

Despite the many spiritual teachers extolling the virtues of meditation, I couldn't meditate. I tried. I went to classes. Invariably, the instructors all cooed: "Let your thoughts go by." One night, sitting in my very best lotus, I saw my frightened thoughts as purple and black blobs scurrying around my head. I cooed: "You can go now." And they did. They got on a train! But as the train pulled away, the blobs looked back at me, leapt out of the windows, and rushed to my side. I gave up. Until I stumbled upon soul writing—a way to meditate *with* my thoughts, my questions, my story. Daily deep soul writing transformed my life from frightened to extraordinary. Along the way, I also fell in love with prayer, walking, and yoga. To me, it's all food. What spiritual practices nourish your life?

NOODLING

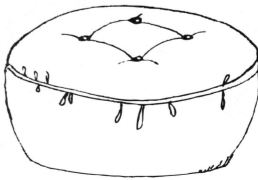

DOODLING & SCRIBBLING

CREATIVE prompt

Close your eyes and scribble-draw for
5 seconds holding this thought: I feel
most at ease when I …
Notice where you are and what you are doing.
Now open your eyes and doodle for 5
minutes to allow more to appear.
More: Close your eyes and do another longer
scribble-draw of 1 minute. Let go of any
thought. Open your eyes and see what
appears this time.

COLORING

DOODLING & SCRIBBLING
Soul Writing

I see ...

You can also meditate visually.
Simply step into your heart
and look around.
What do you see?

DISCOVERING

Dear friends

Aha!

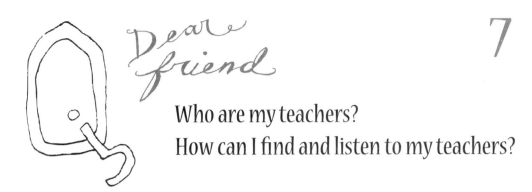

Who are my teachers?
How can I find and listen to my teachers?

On opening night of my courses, I say: *I am not your teacher*. Sound crazy? It makes sense in light of my core belief: *Your answers are within*. I don't have your answers—and neither does anyone else. If you look outside for answers, you'll start following someone else's path when you are here to walk your own. This doesn't mean you don't have teachers. Your life is a brilliant teacher; your soul, a trustworthy compass; your body, a mirror of truth. You are surrounded by messengers, angels, and guides. Your loving divine Voice is a fountain of limitless wisdom, guidance, and grace. There are human teachers, too. Masters and mystics of all traditions have left clues to the extraordinary life. Who are your teachers? Not sure? Invite them and they will come.

NOODLING

DOODLING & SCRIBBLING

CREATIVE prompt

Imagine how your garden would communicate with you. Doodle or scribble the sounds you might hear. Pay attention to the colour it might choose to "talk" to you. Hold your pencil or crayon loosely and notice your heart's guidance on how to move across the page.

More: Draw how the wind in your garden feels when it "talks" to your body.

COLORING

DOODLING & SCRIBBLING
Soul Writing

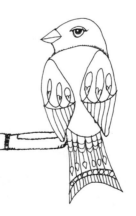

teach me ...

Do you want to invite a teacher?
What clues announce his or her presence?
What do you want to learn?

DISCOVERING

dear Voice

Aha!

Dear Gardener

What feeds my garden?

What feeds my extraordinary life?

As I pull aside the living room curtains each morning, I look at all that's moving in my garden. Once, I followed a subtle wave in the bushes until a pink armadillo emerged! As I close the curtains at night, I wonder, *What moves in the dark?* One night, I stepped outside. The garden in the moonlight is so different from the garden in the sun. As I stared down at my feet, the clear, gentle light of the moon seemed to open the pores of the earth to reveal the garden below the garden. What wonders! Each plant, each tree is supported by a mad bouquet of hungry roots. And the roots are fed by a billion bacteria in each teaspoon of soil! Worms and grubs swim among tiny rivulets in this fertile dark sea. It's a feast down there. A feast! I emerged wondering, *What's feeding me?*

NOODLING

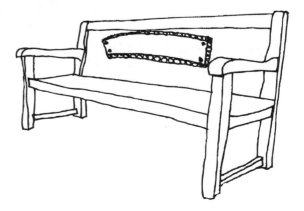

DOODLING & SCRIBBLING

CREATIVE prompt

Get to know your roots. Close your eyes and
imagine standing barefoot with your feet
on the Earth in your garden. See, feel, hear,
and smell the hidden life. *Take a few moments
to breathe the images up through your roots.*
Open your eyes and scribble or doodle intuitively
the rhythmic shapes of the roots as they dance
with the moon. Imagine the shapes as they
intersect each other, feeding what's above.
*More: Look at where your roots intersect. Can you
make out images within the outlines? Doodle to bring
them to life.*

COLORING

DOODLING & SCRIBBLING
Soul Writing

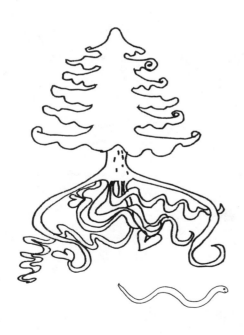

I'm hungry

Look at your roots…
What is feeding you?
Supporting you?
Draining you?

DISCOVERING

Dear? Beloved

Aha!

dear Voice

Who is visiting my garden?

What do my visitors want me to see or hear or feel or know?

My garden is a wee thing, not much bigger than my living room. But to her visitors, she must look like a major university—and they are the visiting professors. Butterflies in the fragrant hot pink frangipani teach me joy. Giant yellow grasshoppers flex their impossible legs, mimicking my own next leap. Squirrels leap through the air to the dove's birdfeeder, reminding me to take more risks in my writing. Osprey soothes me from above as she calls out "Fear not!" Woodpecker once pecked a hole outside my office window and didn't stop until I finished my proposal! And Snake? When Snake arrives, I *really* listen because she is the herald of change. I ask all my visitors to tell me why they've come. And I learn something magical and important from each.

NOODLING

DOODLING & SCRIBBLING

CREATIVE prompt

Close your eyes and imagine seeing a plant in
your garden from the perspective of a grass-
hopper or a bee. Breathe in the image. Really
try to "see" it. Then, open your eyes and scribble
or doodle the plant you saw. If you didn't see
one, allow yourself to scribble one into existence
right now.
*More: Draw an imaginary insect. Then, using your
nondominant hand, draw the trail this insect might
leave behind.*

COLORING

DOODLING & SCRIBBLING
Soul Writing

Hello!

When a creature visits your garden—
physical or imaginal—ask:
Tell me why you're here.
Doodle or soul write their answer.

I'm here to remind you...

DISCOVERING

Dear soul

Aha!

dear
Gardener

What weeds are growing in my life?
How shall I remove them?

Gardens have one problem—weeds. Ignore them, and they become *hard* to remove. The best time is after a good rain. It stormed last night, so today I pulled weeds. In the wet earth, they came up easily, taproot and all. Looking at the roots, I remembered my nemesis weed—jealousy. As a new writer, I struggled with jealousy. Until the day my writing mentor called. She was racked with jealousy over a friend whose manuscript sold for a million dollars. But then, she talked about how long and hard he had worked, and she resolved to be happy for him. I hung up and sobbed: *I will not be jealous. Remove this from me now!* As I cried, the green sludge of jealousy slid out of my heart, down my legs, and into Mother Earth. I was free—free to celebrate everyone's success.

NOODLING

DOODLING & SCRIBBLING

CREATIVE prompt

Draw a circle in the middle of your paper
representing you. Doodle a series of wavy lines
from the edges of the circle outward. Imagine
each of these lines is a weed in your garden.
What colours are they? What do they look like?
Around each weed scribble-draw how they
make you feel. Use the colours that will help
you pull these weeds out by their roots.
More: Draw or name your garden helpers
who know how to eradicate your
weeds for good.

COLORING

DOODLING & SCRIBBLING
Soul Writing

weeding time ...

Is there something you want removed
right now?
Say it. Scream it. Sob it.
Then, pull it out—taproot and all.

DISCOVERING

Dear friend?

Aha!

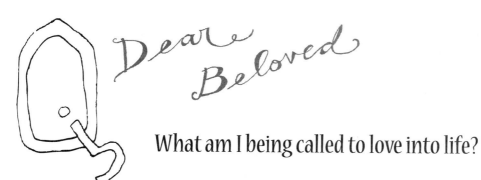

What am I being called to love into life?

I stepped outside on March 4 and noticed a dove—Sophia—sitting on her nest above my back door. Mourning doves lay two eggs that hatch in fourteen days and fledge in sixteen. Could this be? Would Sophia's babies fly on April 1—the very day my next baby, *Soul Vows*, would enter the world? In soul writing I asked, "Sophia, as we give birth to our babies, what wisdom, what guidance, do you have for me?" She wrote, "Trust the birth process. You are to sit on your nest, nourish your baby, and trust the wind. You are the servant mother, the loving mother." On April 1, her nest was empty and *Soul Vows* was in stores! Sophia continues to teach me. And I continue to listen. She has taught me many things; none more important than how to love.

NOODLING

DOODLING & SCRIBBLING

CREATIVE prompt

Draw several egg shapes on your page in
pencil. With your eyes closed and feet flat
on the ground, breathe in and out slowly
three times. Open your eyes and ask the
first egg to tell you what you are nurturing
and caring for inside. Repeat for each egg,
carefully choosing your colour and medium.
Colour each of your precious eggs with pattern,
images, or decorate with words.

More: Draw a picture of you as the mother bird.

COLORING

DOODLING & SCRIBBLING
Soul Writing

my eggs - - -

Close your eyes.
See Sophia on a nest in your heart.
Ask her to teach you how to be a loving mother.

DISCOVERING

Dear friend

Aha!

dear Voice

12

More of this... Less of that...
Where do I want to put my focus?

Each year, I teach six multi-week telecourses, host a weekly radio show, lead retreats, write at least one book—and market it all. To keep up, my lists began to have lists. So, I drove to St. Michael's Shrine in Tarpon Springs, Florida, for guidance. As I poured my litany of obligations onto the page, my beloved divine Voice cut me off: "Stop it! You have *three* things to do: Love your holy God. Love your holy son. Love your holy work." Well, that was clear! The next day, I began to practice the art of *No*. *No*, I can't go to lunch. *No*, I can't talk now. *No*, I'm not going shopping. I rearranged my priorities, pared away the extraneous, and focused on what is sacred for me. A funny thing happened: I fell madly in love with my life, I had all the time I needed—and I got a lot more sleep!

NOODLING

DOODLING & SCRIBBLING

CREATIVE prompt

Lay your hand and forearm down
on your paper. Trace it, imagining your
arm is the trunk and your fingers are the
branches. Fill your branches with leaves, but
before you do take a moment to consider
which leaves are part of your blossoming
and which can be pruned away. Use
whatever colours feel good for your
imaginal leaves. You may want to
name the leaves.
*More: Draw and name the discarded
leaves scattered on the ground
around your tree.*

COLORING

DOODLING & SCRIBBLING
Soul Writing

what's sacred ...

Where do I spend my time?
What is important? Sacred?
What shall I say *NO* to?

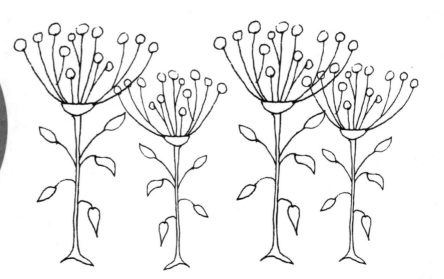

DISCOVERING

Dear? Beloved

Aha!

13

Dear soul

Who shows up to remind me that I am loved?

My father *loved* cardinals. Even on the most bitter Wisconsin day, he traipsed through the snow to refill their feeder. He watched them for hours from his chair in the dining room. He even made a cardinal the logo of his business. So when my father died, I wasn't surprised when a red cardinal chirped outside my dining room window one evening. I said, "Hello, Dad. I love you, too!" A year after my mother died, I heard Dad at the window as usual. "Hello, Jay!" I called. Then I asked, "Where's Laurene?" An orange female flew into the bush. Now, they always come as a pair. They chirp, and I return their love. When I tell my story, people tell theirs: dragonflies, ladybugs, feathers, birds, pennies… We have so many visitors from the other side reminding us that love never dies.

NOODLING

DOODLING & SCRIBBLING

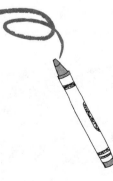

CREATIVE prompt

You may already have a symbol a loved one
sends as a message. If you do, doodle or draw
it, paying attention to what colours you are
using to bring the message to life. If you don't,
close your eyes and bring to mind the last
happy dream you had. Illustrate the dream
using the first 3 symbols that come to mind.
*More: Turn your page upside down. Doodle any
images or ideas you see from this new perspective.*

COLORING

DOODLING & SCRIBBLING
Soul Writing

love alive

Does some*thing* show up often
or in unusual ways?
Is some*one* reminding you
that you are loved?

DISCOVERING

Dear soul

Aha!

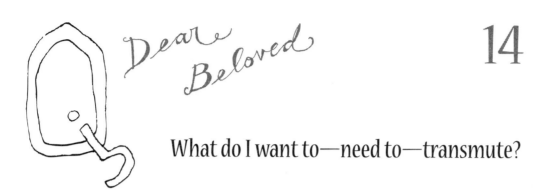

Dear Beloved

14

What do I want to—need to—transmute?

After the divorce, my eight-year-old son and I lived in a dim first-floor apartment filled with dreary furniture. As I opened the door one afternoon to pick him up from school, a baby gray snake, no bigger than a pencil, crawled onto our threshold. "Oh, my son will love you," I said, "Please stay." And it did. They played together for hours. I went inside to make dinner. Suddenly my son screamed. I raced outside. The snake was shedding its skin! This was not an accident. Snake carries the medicine of transmutation—down-to-your-toes change. I knew Snake was asking me to transmute my *toxic* thoughts, words, and actions. And I did. That snake was the harbinger of my extraordinary new life. If Snake shed her skin on your threshold, what would she be asking you to change?

 NOODLING

DOODLING & SCRIBBLING

CREATIVE prompt

You can do this exercise with your eyes open or closed.
Imagine you are the snake shedding its skin.
Choosing a crayon or oil pastel for this exercise will help you
feel the scrape against your paper. With the crayon or pastel
in your nondominant hand, trace the path a snake might
take to shed its old skin. Try to feel the edges of what
your snake would use to pull its skin off.
Feel the satisfaction of letting go.
*More: Draw the "obstacles"—rocks, tree bark,
rough ground—that helped your
snake pull off its old skin.*

COLORING

DOODLING & SCRIBBLING
Soul Writing

NEW Me Coming Soon...

changes...

What thoughts do you want to change?
What words?
Is there something you want
to stop doing?

DISCOVERING

Dear Beloved?

Aha!

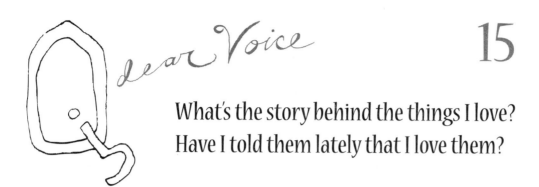

dear Voice

What's the story behind the things I love?
Have I told them lately that I love them?

When *Writing Down Your Soul* came out, I crisscrossed the country speaking and teaching. By summer, I was exhausted. My publicist *ordered* me to shut the computer for five days! I had no money, so I created an at-home retreat of silence, reading, soul writing, long walks, and lush dinners. The first day, I looked up from a book and smiled at my favorite painting. I began to tell her where I saw her, who painted her, and why I love her. I went around the room loving my chartreuse sofa, my mother's crystal, the Green Man from my son, the ghost rock I found on an Oregon beach…. And if I didn't love something, it went straight to the garage. By the end of the day, my heart overflowed with love and gratitude for everything in my life. I still tell my precious things, *I love you*!

NOODLING

DOODLING & SCRIBBLING

CREATIVE prompt

Create a giant flower by gathering images, textures or colours from magazines.
Cut out a special image to represent you and paste it in the middle of your paper.
Cut out several petals from the images you have gathered, paying attention to the
colours that are feeding your heart right now.
*More: Create a second flower collage representing what grows in your imaginal garden.
Each petal can represent what you want to grow there.*

COLORING

DOODLING & SCRIBBLING
Soul Writing

I love you

How does it feel to say
"I love you!"
to your favorite cup?
A cherished memento?
Your sweet home?

DISCOVERING

Dear soul

Aha!

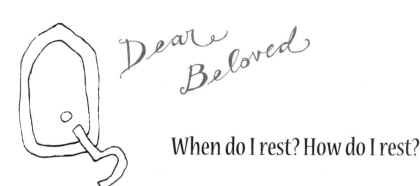

When do I rest? How do I rest?

After my at-home retreat, I felt refreshed and ready to dive back into my work. I resolved to hold on to the feelings of gratitude and peace, but quickly the go-go pace zapped me and I was hungry—desperate—for another day off. So I did it. I turned off the computer and phone and gave myself a whole day of *nothing*. I figured if God rested after creating the world, I could rest after my efforts, too. I grabbed my journal, a new book, and a glass of ice water with lemon and plopped myself on the comfy chaise lounge in my garden. I read a bit and wrote a bit, but mostly I watched the dramas unfolding before me: bees on the hunt, lizards in love, spiders weaving genius, squirrels racing on the power lines. I breathed sky, smelled sun, and resolved to rest again—soon.

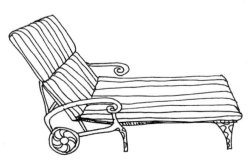

NOODLING

DOODLING & SCRIBBLING

CREATIVE prompt

Close your eyes and take a few long, deep breaths. Someone has put a flyer on the gate leading to your imaginal garden. The flyer says FOUND in large letters and underneath is a picture of a …

Open your eyes and doodle or draw what was found.

More: If you took a day of rest in your imaginal garden, where would you rest? Draw that chair, hammock, or chaise lounge. What colour is it? What is it made of? Who made it?

COLORING

DOODLING & SCRIBBLING
Soul Writing

rest ...

What would a day of rest look like?
Feel like?
Pick a date.
Give yourself the gift of rest.

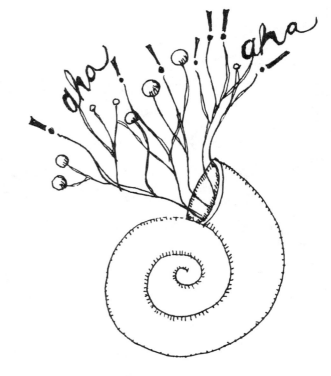

DISCOVERING

Dear? Beloved

Aha!

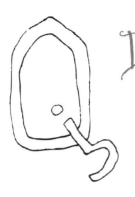

Dear soul

17

How does the sun nurture my life?
Do I honor her faithful gifts?

At three, my son was a stegosaurus for Halloween and would *not* take the costume off. His toys, clothes, and books were all dinosaur-centric. No fireman for him; he was going to be a *pay-wee-o-tah-o-jist*. There was one great sorrow in his love affair with dinosaurs: their extinction when a meteor hit the earth and sent up a dust cloud obliterating the sun. In the long, cold dark, entire species of animals, insects, and plants disappeared. As my sweet boy mourned this irreparable loss, I found myself looking up at the sun and seeing her—really seeing her. The Sun nurtures life. The Sun gives life. The Sun is life. Everything and everyone is possible because the Father Sun returns, without fail, to bless Mother Earth. I stop now, once a day, look up, and kiss the sun.

NOODLING

for E & J

DOODLING & SCRIBBLING

CREATIVE prompt

Draw or trace a circle in the middle of
your page. This is your imaginal garden's
sun. Close your eyes and imagine you can
feel the warmth of this sun on your face.
Feel how it is nurturing you and all life in
your garden. What colour or colours is your
sun? Open your eyes and colour in your
sun, then add radiating circles of
colour around it representing
its healing powers.
More: Give your sun a nose,
mouth, and eyes.

COLORING

DOODLING & SCRIBBLING
Soul Writing

eating the sun

Food is sunlight.
Amazing, isn't it!
Write a blessing
that honors the gifts of the sun.

DISCOVERING

Dear friend

?

Aha!

dear Voice

18

Is there enough in my universe?
Am I enough?

When I'm reading, I often gaze out the window as my mind digests something. The other day, I caught myself staring at a small brown lizard on the patio. She was motionless, as if waiting for me to notice. And notice I did. I suddenly realized her entire life takes place in my backyard. My garden is her universe—and a perfectly contained, utterly vast one at that. She has everything she could possibly want: an endless supply of bugs to eat, raindrops to drink, pavers to warm her belly, sun to warm her back, bushes to hunt in, mates aplenty, and secret places to lay her eggs and welcome the next generation—all in the vibrant green universe of my garden. In her stillness, I heard Lizard say: *Do you see? I have enough—and you do, too. I am enough—and you are, too.*

NOODLING

DOODLING & SCRIBBLING

CREATIVE prompt

Draw a large leaf shape which takes up most of
your paper. Using a soft pencil, scribble-draw
random patterns within the leaf. Let them
crisscross each other. You can do this with
your nondominant hand if you prefer. Take
a look at the shapes you have made and see
what images arise. Doodle or colour to bring
them to life.

*More: Draw the outline of a small creature in your
garden reminding you that you are enough. Doodle
its pattern of completeness.*

DOODLING & SCRIBBLING
Soul Writing

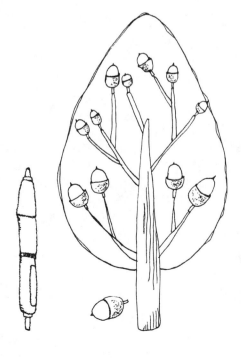

enough.

Be very still for a moment.
Look around inside and outside.
Do you see enough?
Ask sweet Lizard to teach you to see.

DISCOVERING

Dear friend

Aha!

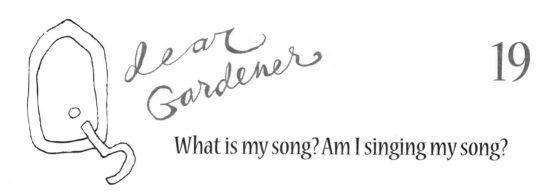

What is my song? Am I singing my song?

I awoke yesterday to a pre-dawn recital. An unknown bird stepped onto center stage below my window, opened her throat, and sang a soprano welcome to the sun. I listened until she took her bow. Soon, a second performance began in a lower register, more staccato, almost danceable. Then the finale: A pair of songbirds inches from my pillow wove their two melodies into one ecstatic chorus of joy. I got up. I felt I was being called to step into my garden and listen for her song. At first, I heard with my human ears, but then I asked my heart to open to the sounds we cannot hear: plants breathing, insects walking, dew drying, pebbles sighing. As I stood there, I realized everyone and everything is singing its song. And every song matters. So I began to sing mine.

NOODLING

DOODLING & SCRIBBLING

CREATIVE *prompt*

Close your eyes and imagine you are lying on your back in your garden looking up at the clouds. Scribble-draw for 5 seconds, trying to capture the sound of those clouds. Open your eyes and doodle the images you saw. Is there a song there? What colour is it? How does it move? Keep doodling. *More. Turn your page upside down and doodle more melodies from your clouds or start a new chorus.*

COLORING

DOODLING & SCRIBBLING
Soul Writing

listen

Stop for a moment and listen.
Consider all you cannot hear.
Imagine the full symphony of life—
including your precious and
important note.

DISCOVERING

Dear soul

Aha!

20

What bounty am I harvesting in my life?

To all gardens the time of harvest must come. It's the cycle of life. The seed, fed by the rain and kissed by the sun, wants nothing more than to fulfill her destiny. The peach to give more peaches. The rose to offer her scent. Bony wisteria to celebrate her climb with ecstatic purple cascades. In my wee garden, sprigs of rosemary, tarragon, and chives lean into my scissors, happy to bless my dinner. Tonight, I held a small green bouquet to my nose and wondered what else wants to be harvested. The sweet cover of this *Soul Discovery Coloring Book* popped into my mind. Oh! I see. She is telling me she is ready to be clipped from *my* garden, so she can blossom in *yours*. The time of the harvest is at hand. What is ripe and ready in your life to be plucked and given away?

NOODLING

DOODLING & SCRIBBLING

CREATIVE prompt

Scribble-draw a giant heart that almost fills your page. Imagine this heart is a cornucopia overflowing with what you have harvested in your imaginal garden. Use texture, colour, words you draw or magazine cutouts to fill it to bursting.

More: Draw a fruit tree. Label each juicy imaginal fruit with the gifts you are harvesting.

COLORING

Thanks to Diego Rivera for the inspiration.

DOODLING & SCRIBBLING
Soul Writing

this is for you

Do you have some fruits to give away?
Who would love to receive your bounty?

DISCOVERING

Dear? Beloved

Aha!

Dear soul

21

What shall I celebrate in the garden of my life?

Our ancient ancestors didn't have computers or books; yet they knew something that we, with all our education, somehow forgot. They knew how to celebrate. Oh sure, we celebrate, but only on the big dates and invariably with effort, expense, and stress. But our ancestors gathered in simple spontaneous celebrations of everything that mattered to the community. This memory tapped me on the shoulder while I was writing my first book. I felt the need one evening to honor what I'd accomplished that day, so I made dinner for one and raised a glass in gratitude to my invisible writing guides. What fun, and what a discovery: Celebration isn't work at all; it's a joy-filled spiritual practice—and one that wants to be woven into our days. What will you celebrate today?

NOODLING

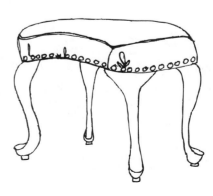

CREATIVE *prompt*

Draw or trace a small circle at the center of your page. This is your celebratory campfire. Now draw or trace a larger circle surrounding the small one. Close your eyes and imagine who is celebrating with you. Open your eyes and draw a shape or colour around your campfire circle to represent all those celebrating with you.

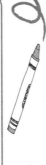

COLORING

i celebrate the magic in ti

p.s. the blank space is for you to add what you're celebrating

DOODLING & SCRIBBLING
Soul Writing

celebrate

Look at your garden.
(Never mind any flaws.)
What wants to be celebrated?
Let the joy begin!

DISCOVERING

Dear soul

Aha!

Dear Beloved

22

What discoveries am I carrying in my heart?

As we step into our final exploration together, I feel happy-sad. Creating this unusual discovery book for *you* has been a heart-expanding experience for *me*. I, too, opened my gate, selected my seeds, fed my roots, and wrestled with a few weeds. I felt you beside me as I kissed the sun, sang my song, realized I was enough, and celebrated my harvest. I felt your presence and I feel it still. In this extraordinary realm, we doodle and write and color as one. That's my big AHA. That and realizing just how deeply we are loved by this great mystery called life. With those two discoveries tucked in my heart, I shall not say good-bye. Instead, I send waves of gratitude for welcoming Christine and me into your extraordinary life. May your garden ever flourish with wonder and joy.

NOODLING

DOODLING & SCRIBBLING

CREATIVE prompt

Go outside for this last exercise if possible.
Plant your feet firmly on the ground. Breathe in
through your feet. Which of the images that you
created needs more expression? Close your eyes and
ask your heart to show you what your final doodle
should be. Or just give thanks for all you have been
shown. Draw *Thank YOU* in big bubble letters and
decorate with hearts, flowers, and joy-filled colours.
*More: Draw a line of Tibetan-style prayer
flags set with your own positive intentions.
Send them out onto the wind
with gratitude.*

COLORING

DOODLING & SCRIBBLING
Soul Writing

in my heart

Look back at your *Ahas*.
Pick the very special ones
and tuck them in your heart.

DISCOVERING

Dear? Beloved

Aha!

To Our Readers

Conari Press, an imprint of Red Wheel/Weiser, publishes books on topics ranging from spirituality, personal growth, and relationships to women's issues, parenting, and social issues. Our mission is to publish quality books that will make a difference in people's lives—how we feel about ourselves and how we relate to one another. We value integrity, compassion, and receptivity, both in the books we publish and in the way we do business.

Our readers are our most important resource, and we appreciate your input, suggestions, and ideas about what you would like to see published.

Visit our website at *www.redwheelweiser.com* to learn about our upcoming books and free downloads, and be sure to go to *www.redwheelweiser.com/newsletter* to sign up for newsletters and exclusive offers.

You can also contact us at *info@rwwbooks.com*.

Conari Press
an imprint of Red Wheel/Weiser, LLC
65 Parker Street, Suite 7
Newburyport, MA 01950